R IVER

OLD NORTH CHURCH

PAUL REVERE HOUSE

KING'S CHAPEL

FANEUIL HALL

OLD STATE HOUSE

OLD SOUTH MEETING HOUSE

LONG WHARF

THE BOSTON TEA PARTY

OLD BOSTON

HEAR YE OF BOSTON

Hear Ye

# of Boston

by Polly Curren

Pictures by Kurt Werth

LOTHROP, LEE & SHEPARD CO., INC. • NEW YORK

I can still remember how confused I was when I first began to study American history. There was so much going on in so many places—and all at the same time. So I decided to choose one place and write a book telling only what happened there, and then move on to another place and tell about the same events happening *there*. Then on again to others—until I had told the entire story of how our nation began and grew. And so I started with Boston—which is the proper place to start.

—*Polly Curren*

Boston is a city,
a big important city.
A stately,
old-fashioned, prim and proper,
full of history city—
this is Boston.
Her streets are narrow—they twist and turn—and
everyone gets lost in Boston.
Her houses are tall and stately.
Some of her sidewalks are made of red bricks.

And right in the middle of the city is the Boston Common,
where once the cows were allowed to graze.

And right beside that is the beautiful Public Garden.

Small colorful fishing boats crowd her famous fish pier.
Big ships from faraway places sail into her broad harbor.
Her port has become one of the largest
on the Atlantic seacoast.

Trains, trucks, buses and cars come and go
through this busy city,
and giant jets zoom overhead.

Hundreds of years ago,
Boston was very different.

She had deep forests filled with wild game.
She had fine soil—rich and dark.
She had salt waters filled with sweet fish.
Her people were Indian—peaceful and friendly.
There were tiny Indian villages tucked here and there,
and happy Indian children played in old Boston.

But soon the world began to march toward Boston.
One June day, in 1630, John Winthrop came from England,
bringing a group of English friends with him.

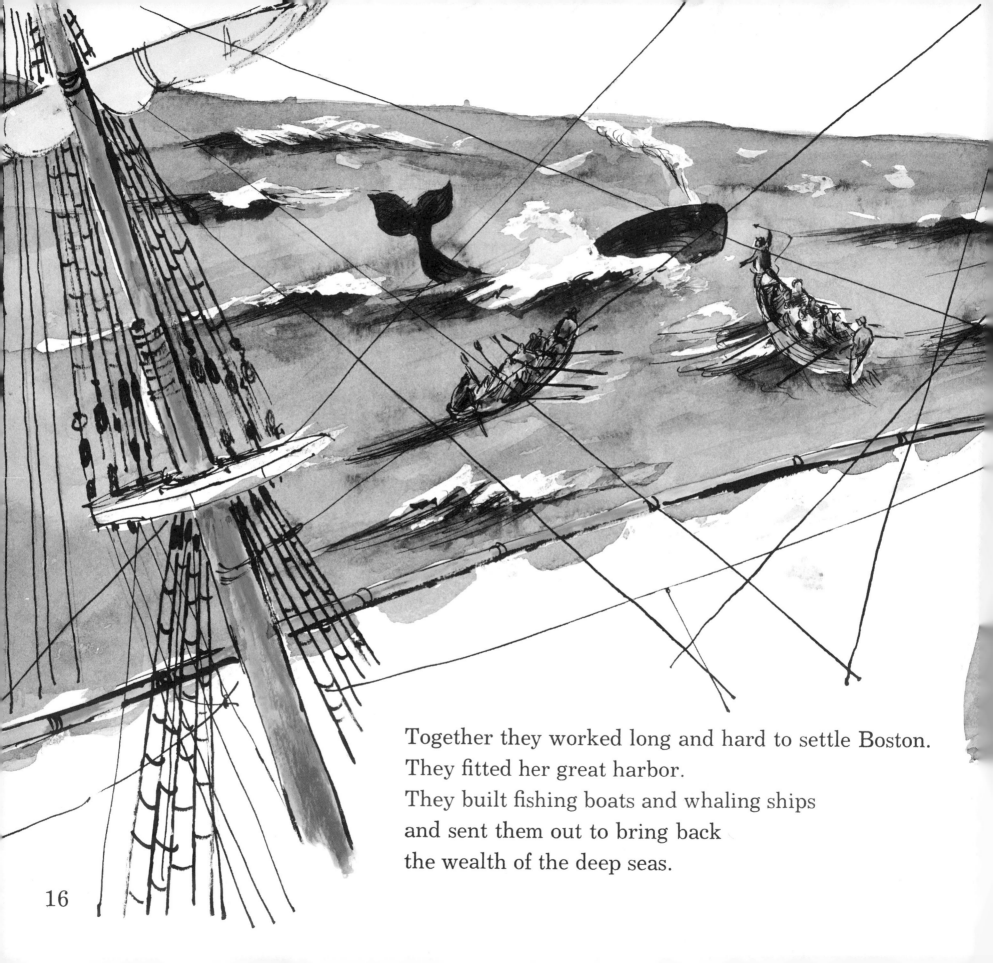

Together they worked long and hard to settle Boston.
They fitted her great harbor.
They built fishing boats and whaling ships
and sent them out to bring back
the wealth of the deep seas.

16

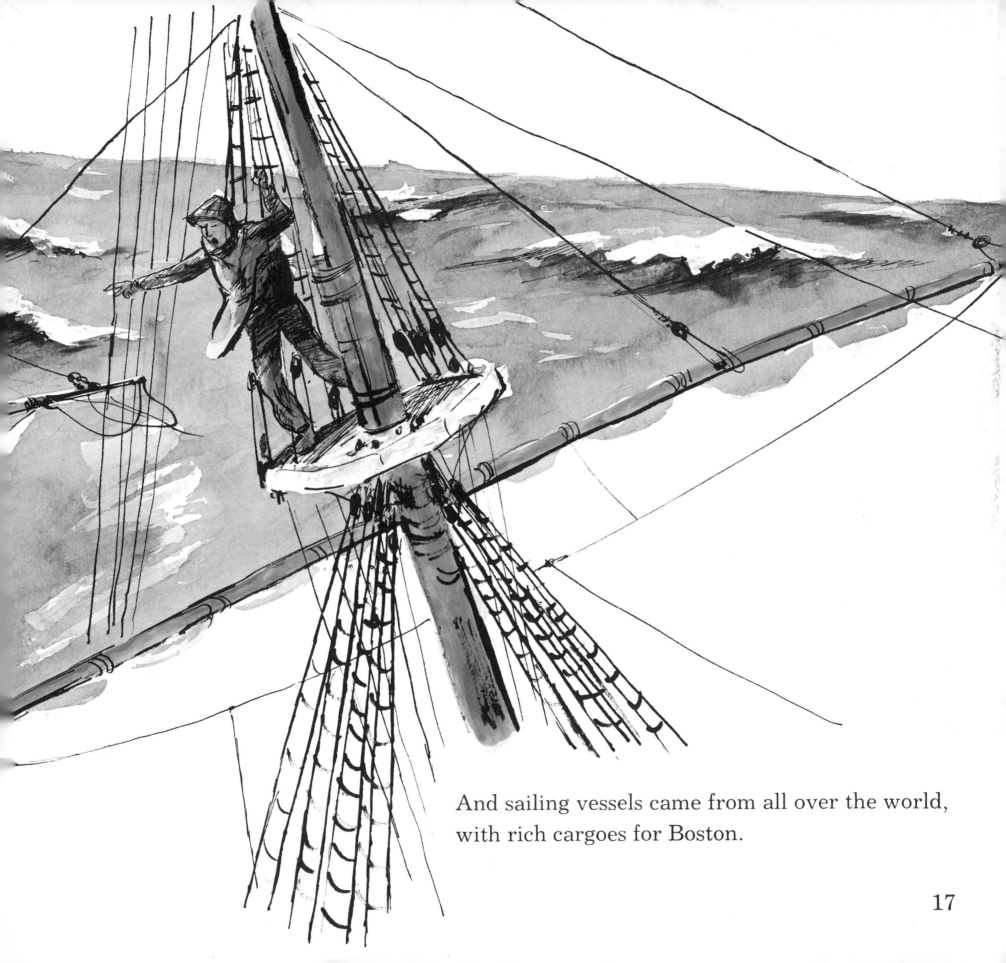

And sailing vessels came from all over the world, with rich cargoes for Boston.

17

They laid out her narrow crooked streets.
Homes were built on three of Boston's hills.
One hill became Beacon Hill.
One hill became Dorchester Heights.
And a third hill became Charlestown.

Boston wanted all her people
to have a fine education.
In 1635, only five years after the city was founded,
the Boston Public Latin School was started.

A Post Office was opened in 1639.
And in 1653, a Library was founded.

Boston was a proud city—a rich city—a happy city.

But then King George the Third of England
began to make trouble for Boston.
Great Britain still owned this part
of the New World, and King George
wanted some of the riches of Boston.

So he levied unfair taxes on all the goods
that came into and left Boston Harbor.
This was the Townsend Act.
He declared a duty on all paper—
newspapers, ships' papers,
even playing cards.
This was the Stamp Act.

And then—King George
moved some of his British soldiers
into old Boston.
The people of Boston did not like British
soldiers living in their city
and they grew unhappy and restless.

At last—in 1770—some British soldiers
fired into a group of people,
and five Boston men were killed.
This was the Boston Massacre.

When three British ships came into Boston Harbor,
loaded with tea, the Boston people refused to buy it.
They even refused to unload it.

And so—on a dark December night in 1773—some of
Boston's leading citizens dressed up like Indians and
stole aboard the darkened ships in Boston's harbor—
and dumped all the tea into the ocean.
This was the Boston Tea Party.

After that King George closed the Port of Boston
to all shipping.
He would not take away the high taxes.
He would not call his soldiers home to England.
So—Boston began to fight.

A few brave men held secret meetings in hideaway places.
They gathered guns and gunshot—
and hid them safely in Concord.
And they decided on a signal
that would warn everyone
if the British tried to attack.
One lantern, hung high in the steeple
of the Old North Church,
would mean the British
were coming by land.
Two lanterns would mean
they were coming by sea.
All men, young and old,
were ready to fight at a moment's notice
for the freedom of Boston.
They were the Minutemen.

The British soldiers watched—and waited.
When they discovered the Minutemen's guns were hidden
a few miles away in Concord, they decided to go and take them.
And on April 18, 1775—the British began to move.

It was a Boston silversmith, Paul Revere,
who saw the signal—two lanterns—
that meant the British were crossing the Charles River in boats,
and would soon begin to march toward Concord.

And it was Paul Revere who rode through the night
to warn everyone that the British
were on their way.

Early the next morning, on April 19, 1775, Minutemen and British soldiers met and fought at a small wooden bridge in Concord.

And *this* first gunfire was the "Shot Heard Round the World,"
the first battle of the American Revolution.
Next came the famous encounter called
The Battle of Bunker Hill, only it was really
fought on nearby Breed's hill.

The next year, on March 17, 1776,
General George Washington,
Commander-in-Chief of the Army,
forced the British to leave Boston.
Then came the triumphant day—July 18, 1776.
The Declaration of Independence
was proclaimed from the balcony of the State House.
The King's Arms and the British flag were taken down
and burned in King's Street.
And now, Boston—brave Boston—proud,
strong and forceful Boston—
was an *American* city,
and began to move forward again.

In the nineteenth century,
more mills and factories
were built along her rivers.
More fine stores were opened
on her narrow twisting streets.
More people came to live
in her fine houses.
They came from Ireland and Italy—
and Poland and Germany—
and many other lands
across the sea.
And they brought their ambitions
and hopes,
their talents and skills,
their courage and their faith,
to help Boston grow.

Boston founded a Symphony Orchestra—

and a Museum of Fine Arts.
And soon Boston became known as
the City of Culture.
Some of her people became famous writers and artists.
And some of her people became
Presidents of their Country.

A fine new State House
with a golden dome was built
on the top of Beacon Hill.
A sky-high tower,
the Bunker Hill Monument,
was built on Breed's Hill in Charlestown,
in memory of the brave men who
fought and fell in battle.

And by the twentieth century
Boston had grown to be one of the largest cities
in the United States of America.

And now Boston, Old Dame Boston, still has

her tall stately houses and
her red brick sidewalks.
Her narrow old streets still twist and turn,
and everyone still gets lost in Boston.
Old Boston Common is still in the middle of the city
but the cows are there no more.
And the Public Garden is still there beside
the Common—more beautiful each year.

Paul Revere's old house
where he made his fine silverware,
the Old North Church
where the lantern was hung,
the place on the sidewalk
where the five Boston men died,
the wharf at the ocean
where the tea was dumped—they all are there, too.
Freedom's trail began
right in the heart of old Boston.

Hear Ye of Boston
was set in 14 point Textype
at Huxley House, New York,
and enlarged photographically.
It was printed at Rae Publishers,
Cedar Grove, New Jersey,
and bound by Charles H. Bohn, New York.

CHARLES

ROXBURY
FLATS

BEACON HILL

STATE HOU

The
COMMON

PAR
CH

R IVER

OLD NORTH CHURCH

PAUL REVERE HOUSE

KING'S CHAPEL

OLD STATE HOUSE

FANEUIL HALL

OLD SOUTH MEETING HOUSE

LONG WHARF

THE BOSTON TEA PARTY

OLD BOSTON